Magnificat
poems

Magnificat
poems

by
Russell Rowland

Encircle Publications, LLC
Farmington, Maine USA

Magnificat ©2023 Russell Rowland

Paperback ISBN-13: 978-1-64599-444-2
Kindle ISBN-13: 978-1-64599-445-9

All rights reserved. No part of this book may be reproduced in any form by any mechanical or electronic means including storage and retrieval systems without express written permission in writing from the publisher. Brief passages may be quoted in review. Rights to individual poems remain with author.

Editor: Cynthia Brackett-Vincent
Book and book cover design: Eddie Vincent/ENC Graphics Services
Cover photo: Colleen Eliason
Author photo: Ann Welch

Sign up for Encircle Publications newsletter and specials
http://eepurl.com/cs8taP

Mail Orders, Author Inquiries:
Encircle Publications
PO Box 187
Farmington, ME USA 04938
508-951-1996

Online orders:
encirclepub.com

in memory of William Stafford
the mentor I never met

*At sight of angels or anything unusual
you are to mark the spot with a cross.*

Acknowledgements

Some of the poems first appeared, often in earlier form, in the following publications:

Amethyst Review: "Annunciation"; "Learning Late."

Bookends Review: "Ties That Bind."

California Quarterly: "Belonging to the Sky"; "Pristine."

Connecticut River Review: "It's the Birches."

Freshwater: "Leaf-Peepers"; "Leaving No Trace"; "Specimen Owl."

Gyroscope Review: "Migratory Birds."

Illuminations: "The Why of a Pond."

Loch Raven Review: "High Beams."

Main Street Rag: "Good Listener."

Northern New England Review: "First Frost"; "Shaker Pond."

Passager: "Perspective."

Pinyon Review: "Kite-String."

Penmen Review: "Smart's Brook in Winter."

Plainsongs: "Abandoned Nests."

Poem: "Closed, Quiet Places."

Progenitor: "A Good Stride."

Pudding Magazine: "Blair Covered Bridge"; "To My Daughter About Her Daughter."

Red Coyote: "Fireweed"; "Unoccupied."

Red Eft Review: "Inside the Cloud"; "Young Girl Up an Old Tree."

St. Katherine Review: "Go Out and Play."

Schuylkill Valley Journal: "When Snow Falls from Trees in Sunlight."

Solum Press: "Not Looking for Angels."

Stickman Review: "Bumper-to-Bumper"; "Lupine, Sugar Hill."

Stillpoint Arts Quarterly: "Ice-Over."

Tar River: "Pedagogy."

Third Wednesday: "Swallowtail Butterflies on Mt. Shaw."

Toasted Cheese: "Ignored by a Chickadee."

Tribeca Poetry Review: "Pumpkin Patch."

Typehouse Literary Magazine: "Crow, Sparrow."

U.S. 1 Worksheets: "Goodness Knows...."

Variant Literature: "Patience."

WestWard Quarterly: "Geese Land on Pond"; "Unwanted Company"; "Winter Solstice."

Contents

1.

Geese Land on Pond 3
Pristine. 4
Bumper-to-Bumper 5
Loon Dancer 6
Vigil for Bear 7
I Write Often of the Deer. 8
Unoccupied 9
Migratory Birds 10
Blair Covered Bridge 11
Split Rock 12
High Beams 13
Shaker Pond. 14
Lupine, Sugar Hill 15
Closed, Quiet Places. 16
A Place Apart 17
Inside the Cloud. 18
I Sometimes Think. 19
Quechee Gorge 20
Red-Wings Among the Cattails 21
Swallowtail Butterflies on Mt. Shaw. 22
Elijah, the Devil, and I 23
Don't We Get It? 24
Pumpkin Patch. 25
Fireweed. 26
NH Fish & Game Opens Bear-Hunting Season. 27
Young Girl Up an Old Tree 28
First Frost. 29
Ice-Over. 30
Smart's Brook in Winter. 31
It's the Birches 32

2.

Perspective 34
Temporal Displacement 35
Rain Coming 36
At the Greenhouse 37
Things to Say 38
A Good Stride 39
Playing the Odds 40
Acolyte 41
Annunciation 42
Pantheism 43
Switchbacks 44
Put Them Up a Tree 45
Kite-String 46
Ties That Bind 47
Pedagogy 48
To My Daughter About Her Daughter 49
The Better Part of Valor 50
Goodness Knows... 51
Learning Late 52
Go Out and Play 53

3.

Telling Time 56
Patience 57
Good Listener 58
"But Some Doubted" 59
Binocular Vision 60
When to Head for the Hills 61
Winter Solstice 62
When Snow Falls from Trees in Sunlight 63
Hibernation 64
Heart Defect 65
Specimen Owl 66
Ignored by a Chickadee 67

Abandoned Nests 68
Unwanted Company 69
Overhearing 70
The Why of a Pond 71
Omen in the Woods 72
Leaving No Trace 73
Meaning No Harm 74
Consultation in Season 75
Crow, Sparrow 76
Leaf-Peepers 77
Hanging the Birdhouse 78
What Trees See Coming 79
I With My Loppers 80
Not Looking for Angels 81
A Stumble Looking Up 82
Belonging to the Sky 83
Turning Back 84
Not Turning Back 85
Sky-Writing 86

*Wherever God has sent me,
the meadowlarks were already there.*

—William Stafford

Geese Land on Pond

Skies yield them, as if their splashdown
were of an order higher than most.

And though geese honk instead of hail,
we have awaited, more than we realized,

assurance we are favored the old way—
with a thunderclap of wings.

Visitation happens mostly when overdue,
the need past helping; comes as varied,

evident beauties, sometimes down rays
of sunlight—avenues of descent.

It occurs rarely; guiding star
perhaps only once in the shortest lives.

So while we can, we sing—to magnify
those times we assented: Let it be to us.

Pristine

High in the Belknap Range is a pond
we disparaged with a name it didn't need,
which I won't repeat. At least

it is free of docks and rafts, cabins,
loud motor-craft scratching it with wakes
that heal slow—spared becoming

a traffic-jam like Winnipesaukee,
nearby. All day, every season, the pond
remains a blue lens gazing trustfully,

fond daughter, up at Mother,
blue sky. A nesting heron calls it home;
agile trout make widening splashes.

You see pretty clear to the bottom,
where life waves and wiggles, without one
beer can or castoff fridge—

I know, having stood at the brink
looking deeply, from this reflected face
that the ripples made ridiculous.

You may come up with me,
the day a wedge of geese returns—if so,
you'll come sworn to secrecy.

Bumper-to-Bumper

A lot of summer traffic bound
for the White Mountains passes through here.
It stops at the lights downtown,

and is soon backed up to New Jersey.
Heat rises off cars: they shimmer like mirages
on the pavement that carries them

to North Conway. Hearts like mine
wish something else than what these pilgrims
are after, with their bike racks, Gucci

tote-bags. Our hearts hang around
cellar holes, stone walls, untended graveyards
deep in the woods; follow dirt roads

between oaks to clearings where
the roads just end. We are gone all day, then
walk home with acorns in our pockets.

Loon Dancer

One of a pair, the red-eyed yodeler
rises in the water, wings waving. Territorial
is the dance of April's prolonged hours.

In Meredith Bay it will take a lot
of dances, once the motorboat juggernauts
return—none intending to overrun,
but few on the lookout either.

A spirit akin to loons, you learned
to dance upon your own deep waters, dark
down there, drownings, still yours:
the territory you have to swim or sink,

despite the prow's endangering wake.
You can only dance your claim. The rest
is up to them and their horsepower.

I have a little cellar hole of my own,
up in the Ossipees overlooking the water,
no walls, no roof—but I will dance,

when they come with chainsaw or campfire
to that second-growth clearing. I will
do the dance of loons to the boater,
Poles to the Panzer. It does not prevent

what happens next—yet as we fly,
displaced, at least we can say we danced.

Vigil for Bear

A man walking his beagle reported seeing bear
ahead in the woods, so Ann and I walked
up that trail a little way: interested, unafraid,

to sit on a log in the area the man described;
perhaps be granted the same epiphany—
which proved not to be, though we were quiet.

Second-growth was a city pleased with where
it was, no need to regret reclaiming
once-farmed-over uplands in the Ossipees.

We watched the woods watch us, a dialogue
of eyes toward consensus without
debate. Bear probably, yet out of sight.

We didn't complain, went unpursued
the way we came, and left little behind except
lingering scents for bear to interpret.

I Write Often of the Deer

Their slender silhouettes
cross my mind stealthily
like cloud or dream and I
try hard not to bolt them

They cannot appreciate
my tributes yet might
find crisp pages palatable
in the absence of forage

They have lineage but
no literature they do not
know our language just
our gunfire

I write often in pursuit
of that which crosses
the high ridge of knowing
at wisdom's horizon

encoded in the hoofprints
of their shadowy passage
through embodiment amid
the stockade of hardwood

Their endangered secret
I still hope to discover but
would keep regardless lest
they diminish in the telling

Unoccupied

All over town, houses languish untenanted,
doors wide open, in fact no doors at all,
because it is winter, and these are birdhouses.

I haven't noticed any agent's signs,
listings in the realty section of the newspaper.
Again, they're birdhouses, and it is winter.

The market waits. A northward sun
will bring clients, flocks of them—then we
should see some rivalry over lodging.

Accommodation of the fittest. For now,
this season of stillness, there lies among us
an abandoned city not ours to populate.

One's heart goes out to the tiny boxes,
empty of all but hope, and like some people
we pray for, created to be forsaken.

Migratory Birds

Cedar Waxwings in nascent foliage
flocked beside Hawkins Brook yesterday,
gone today—lines of longitude not
in any atlas, only in avian printed circuits.

Long lines up the continent, reversible
under heaven. Traffic south and north,
Eden to Armageddon.

I see the lifeline on my palm extend itself
out of the familiar into the unsettled,
like kite-string with its papery wings hid
at hazy height. But tugging.

Migration of souls is also a matter
of two habitats, leagues of sky between:
love one terminus, death the other.

There wasn't time to ask the Waxwings
which is nearer, if migrants know.
What could they say: Just come, just go.

Blair Covered Bridge

Stressed trusses bear our better angels
over the obstreperous Pemigewasset,
bound for the Merrimack on business
strictly riparian. A roof spares us sky
that holds our evanescence over us.

We respect the six-ton rule, one saint
at a time. Eastbound and westbound
chariots alternate—decently, in order,
here in Campton as above in heaven;
as long ago, before Babel, confusion.

At All-Hallows, a cloud of witnesses
pass over as they did alive: memories
of sheep on hillsides, church socials,
carefree youngsters in farm wagons,
fresh from picking apples in season;

each wagon cider-scented, creaking.
Wheels still roll today: Sport-Utility,
chromium pickups, vans. The river,
precipitate between alluvial banks,
might as easily be that other, Jordan:

proverbial "one more river to cross,"
houses of open doors on the far side,
continuing commerce of the faithful
who if they cannot do well do good;
and for whose homecoming, bridges.

Split Rock

On one Pemigewasset bank below Blair Bridge
a granite boulder, man-height, is split
down the middle, two cloven sides smooth
as a pared Cortland. Ramsay thinks

the halves move farther apart each spring,
water eating away the bank beneath
the lower one. He thinks it will tumble in,
some spring, ending the relationship.

Water's freeze, thaw, swelling, contraction,
surely perpetrated this fissure in
the first place. Children play Rock, Scissors,
Paper. Water, if included, would win

hands down. It is a player: kayakers
drowned here. But, as love to its marriage,
the bisected boulder holds for now.
We with luck will last long before dying.

High Beams

It was indeed "deer in the headlights"
last night as I drove home from Campton,
but this doe bolted right back
into wooded darkness where cars don't go.

In Campton as I said goodbye, we noticed
a chipmunk flattened to two
dimensions on the road by poor judgment.

Before dawn, I watched twin stars
match a deer's wide eyes in my headlights,
doe escaping to reflect real starlight
rather than two brilliant suns that come

out of nowhere with a rush, then nothing.
I thought of literal sunsets—
how night is meant for concealment, sleep

for songbirds, shadow for furtive creatures
furbearing, clairvoyant. Our own
night drives cross no yellow line. We dim
our beams lest we blind each other.

Shaker Pond

A long walk holding hands
where no one else goes so no
litter or fire-ring smudge to spoil it
almost justifies considering
a pond away in the woods ours

Ownership is complicated
while love has prior claim
State and Conservation Trust
and Forestholdings LLC are
claim-jumpers in the faster lane

What First Folk never dreamed
of owning was once a little brook
God taught to run downhill
and thought it very good a God
not big on tower construction

Shakers coming with oxen yoked
together set bulwark stones
that broadened the flow down
to the snail's-pace of a pond
hands to work and hearts to God

Shakers now extinct from years
of celibacy reengineered a brook
for this millennial couple who
feel rich and God walks here
too not remembering it like this

Lupine, Sugar Hill

Say pilgrimage, and minds leap to Lourdes,
but in June it's to secessionist Sugar Hill
that we process for healing and apparition:

veritable meadows of vernal violet—spiked,
offering us stigmata of vibrant sensation
in place of ennui from glowing screens.

A horde merely follows each new season,
but one amputee on crutches, for instance,
skillful at swinging along, yet different—

her eyes too, can see the profusion ranked
beneath high Franconia Ridge, her phone
bring it back like theirs, the two-legged.

They may esteem themselves able-bodied,
but who needs no cure? Only the blooms
are flawless, partaking of beatific earth;

they alone mend estrangement from it.
As exiles we come to the salutary field,
then home rejoicing, to put down roots.

Closed, Quiet Places

That vernal pool along an Ossipee trail
is now a hollow in the underbrush, papered
with dry leaves. After all, it is summer.

Still, I couldn't avoid suspicion,
passing by today: as if there were potential
for greater activity than appeared—

frogs reunited, peepers in clear voice,
or something novel in the way of lifeforms,
that could change woods and villages.

You know how even stiff-lipped
New England Congregationalists will get
enthusiastic, late March, early April.

The local meetinghouse shut down
ages ago—yet I wonder what is going on
there, or in woodland graveyards, or down

cellar holes. All closed, quiet places,
certain days, are worth keeping an eye on:
they might be where things happen

unlooked-for, things that help us
with our disbelief. I have heard the bell
in the steeple rung by a strong wind.

I've watched a whirlwind stir up
foliage in that vernal pool—like feet, like
someone dancing, someone invisible.

A Place Apart

According to ancient witnesses,
Jesus withdrew often to the wilderness—
to the mountains, to "a place apart"—
and pulled his prayer shawl over his head.

Those are my places, and I hope
that if we meet, he won't go public on me:
we can be just a pair of sparrows
in the same tamarisk tree for a while.

Two looking at one sunset feel it
more deeply—see it in each other's eyes.
If they climb the same mountain,
the Great Spirit greets both at height.

Something in his face might tell me life
is too short for all the mountains there are.

Inside the Cloud

What to say about this morning's fog?
When we reached high trailhead,
all was obscured, the hikers phantoms.
A dog barked we couldn't see.

Driving there, we'd scanned the range
from a distance. One cloud lay
on top of it, like a big fat Merino
waiting to lose us in its fleece.

Friends were invisible ten feet away.
It was like being old in a white room.
Or nodding off. Counting down
under anesthesia for the surgeon.

It looked like the last thing you'd see
before dying. But soon enough day
broke through. We tightened our laces
and went where the sun wanted.

I Sometimes Think

There are cloudless days that caution me
I too must be perfect, as my heavenly Father
is perfect.

Most days one cloud at least,
then more, float past innocently like my little
white lies.

And there are overcast days
when I remember how my sins have found
me out.

I sometimes think the Great Spirit spreads
blue sky as an alternative for those who didn't
read the book.

Once only, when I helped carry a stretcher
down off Mt. Washington, did I find clouds
beneath me.

Quechee Gorge

If the Ottauquechee keeps cutting,
it could yet reach Earth's core, and a cloud
of steam rise, incense from the altar.

Till then, along the banks are ferns,
dandelions, and other ephemera that thrive
in times between cataclysms.

Yes, these are quiet hours. Birds
feed complacently, as if aware they will be
long gone before the next upheaval.

Along the path one couple pushes a stroller
holding the judgement of the world:
their gift against its cycles, six weeks old,

asleep despite the roaring of the rapids.
This one may not now remember
parturition, that catastrophe of Exile;

still is marked by it: to bestride the gorge,
summon us children of the Deluge
to meet the angels of our nature in the air.

Red-Wings Among the Cattails

In these wetlands, cattails lift
their sausage-tops. No Moses
amid such unbiblical bulrushes—

still, Providence supports.
A Red-Winged Blackbird host
says grace in grackle-tongue.

Beaks tease out the cotton
cattails contain, seeking that pearl
of price: a caterpillar Cosmet Moth,

dreaming of its own wings;
late winter's sweet manna
for red-striped aviators.

Hope may disappoint; pickings
fail in adverse conditions. Many
are the eggs that never hatch.

Puritan Reverend Edwards,
after a typical hellish homily,
wrote in gentler humor—

"Have we not heard, have we
not known, how the Spirit
feeds and flocks its own?"

Swallowtail Butterflies on Mt. Shaw

A prolific season to be alive, even if
transitory. They are not existentialists,
just countless chips of sunlight, jittering.

Who will admonish them time is not
eternity? It is not? Or warn of a day
the deathwatch cicada starts to sing.

I am but little lower than angels here,
yet must be cast down, like Lucifer,
with halo of Swallowtails encircling—

envious of so brief an attention span,
innocence of any agenda save to light
on a flower while still sound of wing;

of freedom from forebodings which,
in those who realize the hour is short,
add venom to a yellow-jacket's sting.

Elijah, the Devil, and I

Down Henniker way they have that rock
showing the Devil's Footprint.
You have to search, but it's there,

as if Old Scratch took the step
to remind us it's very tough to be good,
no matter who we blame.

I have left a print of my boot
in the liquid mud of spring runoff—
then watched it fill, disappear.

It might have been a pathway
the First Nations walked, who made
a point of not leaving tracks,

and in the Great Spirit's presence
would wipe their feet. The same Spirit,
upon a time, was not in the wind,

earthquake, or fire, only a still
small voice afterward, questioning
the weather-beaten prophet—

as I have been asked in turn, reaching
the holy ground of a summit—
"What are you doing up here, Russell?"

Don't We Get It?

We miss the peepers.
Yes, a vernal pool was here,
but now it is summer.

Nothing sad about
the Whitten cellar hole.
They moved, that's all.

Bless the dragonflies.
Still, not for our wellbeing
do they chase mosquitos.

This mountain never asked
to bear you-know-who's
name. The tallest oak ahead—
we're standing on its toes.

Pine Warblers, Nuthatches
are confused by twin suns:
lenses of our binoculars.

Painted Trillium was
before the Blessed Trinity.
Closed Gentians
are supposed to be.

Pumpkin Patch

Here, at the patch beside the River Road,
we who could not choose our relatives
may Pick Our Own—nobody but ourselves
to blame for orange wreckage on the ground
if a stem breaks off in transit, or for rot
discovered beneath the blade, belatedly.

O sphere segmented into zones of time,
like earth itself. O slimy tangle of pulp,
with seeds too slippery to grasp—out, out
of the cavity, into the frying pan you go,
October hors d'oeuvres.
                        O tabula orangina,
blank slate awaiting one presentable face,
mask either of comedy or tragedy, as per
the disposition of its carver toward the year.

Children who come for candy after dark
are drawn like moths by a taper burning low
in the recesses I carved. Or is it my soul
they see consumed? Is it All Souls, as on
the day after Halloween? Or all autumn
ablaze—treetops, stubbled fields of corn,

the burning of the mountain down to rock:
insufferable purification—after which
the mask collapses and cannot be worn.

Fireweed

Red Hill stayed recalcitrantly green
during October. November's first sunrise
set it at last on fire. It blazes now.

Since I passed into age, an ancestral spirit
has spoken within my thought. Seeing
red foliage through my eyes, it counsels:

"The Great One has come to his hilltop.
This is the day all trees wait for,

the day of their coming out. They will soon
offer leaves, first-fruits of branches,
as a thanksgiving to the One who has come.

Do not go up there yet, or he
might turn you into fireweed, which appears
on hillsides flames have swept—

you would intoxicate pollinators,
prosper in sunshine that formerly was shade.

Bees could make honey out of you,
widows tea, the farmer's daughter jam."

NH Fish & Game Opens Bear-Hunting Season

"It is more important than ever to be absolutely
sure of your target, and what lies beyond it."

A lot of hikers and their kids are in the woods
these days, so it is more important than ever.

The population of black bears has grown
in recent years, more than usual killed
last year. Be absolutely sure of your target.

The beginning of a four-month stretch
of the year's most popular hunting season,
yet what lies beyond it?

One trail volunteer guesses black bears take
his loppers for a rifle, by the way they bolt—
absolutely sure they are the target.

Are we not all hunters, out of love or lust?
But at that moment of consummation most
desired, take thought to what lies beyond it.

In this season of rage and firepower, wear
hunter's orange in the forest of your life.
It is more important than ever.

Young Girl Up an Old Tree

The stricken pine was caught and held
on its way down, by a good neighbor.

At that angle it was more a staircase
for the child to climb, than a ladder.

She would go home needles and sap,
with Gram's photo from ground level.

In my childhood girls didn't climb trees.
Branches were full of boys, brave ones.

The timid got jeered off, told to go play
with dolls. So yes, we've made progress.

From such an elevation, Gram appeared
foreshortened, belittled, and earthbound.

The girl could see way out to her father,
dot of color on Squam Lake's early ice—

trusting its solidity a half-mile offshore,
the way he did once, a boy, on a dare.

First Frost

Welcome it as an indulgent father
the youngster home loved for his trouble

Rime on the lawn spicules like fingerbones
on every window when you awaken
skin on Shannon Pond till sun shoos it
ducks well aware it will return

Welcome it with that open heart
which receives unexpected company
and wrestles setbacks into godsends

as counseled by Pastor and on texts
in needlepoint hung up in the parlor

Welcome it since to turn away
and slam the door will hardly chasten it
into giving midsummer back

Welcome it graciously you did after all
think to bring the last tomatoes in

Ice-Over

On Shannon Pond this morning
November ice made arabesques
and doilies mallards couldn't help
but notice. They had squandered
autumn there, beaks underwater
and feathered fannies in the air.

Aquatic fowl do seem indifferent
to a constricting circumference:
who's ever seen a worried duck?
Ice-overs needn't concern them.
Without having studied winter,
their wings know when to leave.

And look ahead: homecoming?
That resettled bear in the news
made it back two hundred miles
to Dartmouth, to be a nuisance
all over again: it was little to her,
save for a couple road crossings.

Meanwhile a Great Blue Heron
that stood like a floor-lamp in
the shallows two summers ago
has not been back: an absence
that still preoccupies me, more
than some would think healthy.

Smart's Brook in Winter

Dressed in layers much like us, except
with lengthier robes of ice and snow,
the stream is out of sight, but there.

It has swept away an autumn of leaves,
cleared out jammed tree trunks, even
stripped a moose carcass—good work.

From the highway a foot trail follows:
we seem to seek brooks. Attendance
at their running must encourage ours.

That downstream whisper is a tongue
we would like to master. The sparkle
of its cascades leaves us thirsting less.

Leashed dogs greet each other—wary,
enthusiastic, usually without warfare.
Somehow the brook tames wildness.

My daughter walks it with me. We've
a history: my touch made her different
from others when she wished likeness.

We both share a brook with strangers.
Maybe all started at the same spring,
and go the one way to the same sea.

It's the Birches

After a recent bucket-drop of wet snow,
trunks are ermine-jacketed, upper limbs
glittering candelabras; woodlands buffed
as if expecting the Extraordinary Visitor.

Occasion for squints. As the sun shines,
branches turn lively and begin to shed
their ice-sheaths on your upturned face.

All isn't jubilee. Most of the birch trees
have bent over—they are prone to this—

till their branches catch in moist snow
on the ground and freeze to it. Can't
free themselves. Imagine colonial girls
washing their tresses in a brook that all
at once freezes: there you have birches.

The larger ones arch right over the trail.
Walk, and it seems like your wedding,
everything just as white as you wanted.
Yet at every wedding somebody weeps,
somebody got hurt to make you happy.

It could be that jilted boyfriend or last
girlfriend, possibly the widowed mom
who is losing you. But in the forest
following heavy snowfall, other trees
tossing pale confetti, and the guests
taking photographs—it's the birches.

You learn what you are, but slowly.
—William Stafford

Perspective

I've worked with folks who wished
I was someone else, and am proud to say
I did not accommodate them, content

if each night, a star impossibly far off
entrusted its spark of life to me.

There were bullies early, who got out
of bed angry and came looking—

but aware how long starlight takes
to reach here, I understand how stars
swallowed long ago by some black hole
can still shine for me, like the saints.

You could step out yourself at night,
nothing between you and the Dippers,
The Hunter, The Milky Way, but space,

and quiet. No crying or pain. Do not
take my word, get out and look.

I was once a little boy walking home
in tears over a skinned knee, too young
to know the galaxy was up there, within
the blue, behind the sun: a great clock
that might strike twelve in my lifetime.

Temporal Displacement

Comes a young man, briefcase in hand,
peddling policies door-to-door
for Prudential Hartford. At one house
there has been death: he comes too late.

See him turn away, face flushed—hates
the job. But mark the small child,
his new girlfriend's son and redhaired,
brought along this time, trotting

beside. Does that young man realize
how the redhead adores him? I do—
the episode's survivor, rufus hair
white now and windblown.

Key broken off in lock, grounder
beneath my fielder's glove, an error.
At last he thundered at me: "Russell,
you do everything bass-ackward."

Long past was the way I sold myself
upon introduction when I was three,
available cheap to the right father—
"I am a very good little boy."

Rain Coming

Relentlessly, defenseless blue
is overwritten by galvanic grey,
so charged it surprises nobody

when the forked tongues lick us,
our conducive bones own it,
and Dog goes under bed.

In the Cold War that followed hot,
our town tested that wailing banshee,
the air-raid siren. Mother explained

about bomber-planes. I broke
into tears: "That means bomber-planes
are coming!" "No!" She stamped

her foot, taking poor explanation
out on me—as I had seen little girls do
whom I found incomprehensible.

Today, when I open an umbrella
against the rain, I stand inside a small
safety that feels about right for me.

At the Greenhouse

Boxes of pansies
lined up in rows
outside the greenhouse
eager petal faces guess
Mother's Day is coming

They will go to homes
adopted like puppies
from the Humane Society

three boxes to our house
offerings to appease
a discontent we caused
afternoon shades drawn
not knowing what we did

and no thanks said

All the little faces nodding
excitedly in their boxes
look round at everything

then grow still as they see
the four of us overhead
Something (who knows
what) seems off to them

Things to Say

A brushy knoll behind the house
at road's bend in far-off Bethel
inters Mother's ashes. I suspect
she and the present owners haven't met.

Father hurried his shovel as if
he couldn't wait to turn the marriage under.
Still he paused to glare at the two of us
through his glasses. "Should anything be said?"

Mother had things to say. "Oh Don,
I don't think you know what love is."
To Christopher: "You'll never be any good."
To me: "The doctor told me to do this."

A more forthcoming father might have said:
"Love was a stranger in our house,
the friend I had yet to make."

My brother: "Once never comes and goes,
I will be good with orphans and stray animals."

When it fell to me: "After the years circle
forty times, what was done will be undone."

That day, we let the shovel talk:
a gravelly voice, grating on rock.

A Good Stride

Coiled on a ledge, the copperhead
soaks up sun like a kitten. I respect
its basking, from my higher niche.

Mother and Father, you can't climb
up here beside me—and all
your controversy is settled. I sidle
down to the brook, skirting
the sunlit ledge with its sunbather.

My legs were shorter and slower,
Father, that day you chased me
with a garter-snake squirming in
your hand. I screamed, you giggled.

Mother, you sang, "A tisket, a tasket,
Vera's in the casket." After cirrhosis
took you, we could have tried out
your own song with your name in it.

I have a good pace, a strong stride.
If you two ever reach the brook,
I will already be on the far side
of the mountain between us.

Playing the Odds

Clouds tease us: "30% chance of rain."
If we head for the hills, we could get soaked.
If we stay put, the sun might break through
in cheeky rebuke of us homebodies.

Once I asked the Spirits for direction: how to act
as they would have me in a matter.
The silence was eloquent. Son, we've given you

the wistful White-Throated Sparrow, and a trail
uphill to where it sings. Sent a brook
through your childhood. Helped you figure out

which way geese fly, what side of a tree
the moss grows on. No bushwhacking for you.

Ancestors will walk beside you on the path
you take. Your children will rise up
and bless you, once old enough to understand.
Hear the song. Follow the same brook.

I made my decision, owned it—with
a bird that used its voice, the brook that found
its way, trees that knew where north is.

Acolyte

Above spreadeagled Winnipesaukee, hours spent
in the ring-dike Ossipees (home to an alleged
sacrificial stone), feels like eavesdropping, believe me.

When the shamans and the sachems transitioned
to spirits, a drum invoking the volcano,
heated rocks steaming sweaty bodies in the lodge,

they spoke every dead language then, held counsel
with the moon and sun, even the future. I
would overhear it if I listened and the wind was right.

A Puritan child, I thought of course of defunct saints
walking the streets of Jerusalem after
the graves split, according to our blessed Evangelist;

but this was the Great Spirit moving upon the surface
of Winnipesaukee, troubling its water.
This was many spirits, overrunning our missionaries.

I've asked to be an initiate, undergo the serial ordeal,
and leave my empty skin like a snake upon
the forest floor. But they know that skin is white.

Annunciation

You're nothing and nobody—naturally
downcast, inconspicuous as befits
your nature, flying under the radar—

then, no particular day, there's a flutter,
presence, greeting. Its benediction
sounds intended for somebody else.

You say "No way," or else "Let it be,"
or both. But you will be remembered
by others also elected for no reason.

I never thought to start a line of kind
children, change the mood in a hall
by standing up to speak quietly,
help carry a stretcher out of the woods.

Once, a hawk's shadow passed over
as I loitered along the Ossipee ledges.
I thought, "Gabriel?" And I called,

"Not happening, thank you very much."
The winged shadow circled back.

Pantheism

Love on the ground may be early snow
we awoke to or in spring simply dew
delighted that sunrise found it yet why not
name it Love and go from there

Indigo Bunting in the branches heaven
isn't always that blue so how about
if we call it Thou and see what it answers

When a mouse rises in owl's talons think
bread broken by the priest's hands
In a drop of blood left on snow recognize
the Passover cup lifted in parting

Christen it Death and allow it into
the circle pass it the pipe and settle with it
Let this be a duet sung sweetly

Pond holds ducks to its breast the hills
embracing it more alive than we've realized
like a banner over us or an eye on us

What it sees it becomes and if you measure
that by the kingdom inside you
then you'll start to feel at home anywhere

Switchbacks

Working its way to and fro
up Turtleback, the old carriage road
spared workhorses, under load
of passengers, from dropping dead

in harness. Kindness has benefits.
As for foot-traffic, switchbacks
show how far you can walk
while not getting far from the spot

you started. Distance is relative.
You could have a full life
of thirty-five years, or live to ninety
and be nowhere. Not mine

to judge. Life does its switchbacks.
I left homes, friends, lovers
at every turning; wended my way
up those sidelong gradients

to the top. There was no hurry.
I look back now toward trailhead:
near, as hawks fly. People
there, waving. Faces I recognize.

Put Them Up a Tree

Mother Black Bear gets her cubs
up a bole into low branches at first alarm
involving dogs or rifles.

Heredity teaches, but safety is dubious
once hunters arrive, barrels pointed skyward.
What justifies a futile precaution?

Mother needs that Tree of Life
which grew so lofty, flocks out of the blue
nested in its branches unmolested.

We want it for other mothers'
children, holding their ears as army tanks,
spewing hatred and shells, rumble in.

I want it for little Janet, the aunt
I didn't know: twelve when a half-brother
in carelessness shot her. I'd get Janet

settled on an acclimatizing limb,
her treble mimicking spring peepers as thin
legs swing—left eye intact again.

Kite-String

When the wind loses its temper
(fifty-mile-per-hour rants today)—
especially if you're hiking a ridgeline
you start to reassess gravity
and your own ballast.

I've encountered winds of a mind
to sweep me back to this or that
abandoned childhood home
and leave me there, an orphan—
or blow me off my trail of choice
into some cutthroat profession.

Thus far by nimble footwork
I've kept myself bound to earth—

where tears water a garden,
and laughter redeems the hour
of affliction; where we stumble
into hugs we didn't see coming,
till children arrive—godsends
we never knew we needed.

Here below, love holds against
the gale's tantrum, rides it—tied,
steady to hand—on a kite-string
let out slow, one length at a time.

Ties That Bind

Three nights in a row I've seen
November's Frost (or Beaver) Moon
pause at my window in passing.

Gravity brings it on a lariat
past earthbound me, amid the rodeo
of spheres in the night watch.

I pretend love is involved:
Mother Earth like every wise parent
allows impetus, while holding on.

The girl asked, one wild March:
"If the string breaks, Dad, the kite—
won't it fly away from us?"

From my understanding
of aerodynamics I explained it thus:
how her kite stays airborne

by resistance to the string,
trying to get free of earth and join
prevailing winds by adoption.

After I said so, my ten
fingers tightened on quivering twine:
her own orbit, around my life.

Pedagogy

We introduced our toddler to a Christmas tree,
star at its apex; taught her to say "pretty!"

Next spring, birds will return to tutor her
in blue, red, yellow. Courtesy singing lessons.

Summers, her father will lead her down beside
the Pemigewasset. Show how he skips stones.

Autumn, gold corridors for her and me to walk.
She will find leaves to put on Grampy's head.

In time, her mother can take her shopping
to discover how inflation treats a dollar.

We will watch her eyes widen with the world.
With knowing it. Who thunder is mad at.

Which dogs can be patted. That wildflowers
are not for picking. How brief each day.

Older, she may realize our teaching
concealed a deeper anxiety—to be sure

we had the world right, that our green in fact
was green—that we had never lied to her.

To My Daughter About Her Daughter

We've trapped one more little soul
in infirma nostri corporis, have we not—
like ethereal fireflies you and I caught
(but those we released) in jars of light—

plighted another to know bodily
pleasure and pain; the loves that will
not let go, the loves that will not stay.

She is four, every age on earth
rolled into one, every daughter who
ever lived and ever will—who never
asked embodiment, expecting better.

Watch her there, she's watching us,
learning from us, learning us—
the one lesson not to learn, that we
cannot help but teach.

Soon she will know us best.
Then she will gaze in a mirror,
and notice our faces behind her—
smiling, though contrite.

The Better Part of Valor

If a child asks me whether the Cardinal
knows it is red, I must think a long time
toward a short answer.

Discretion is needed in deciding what
to tell or not tell a trusting child about
things you don't know.

The child in question, six now, learns
fast: the color of things, and inevitably
in time Grampy's shortcomings.

Maybe suggest she ask the bird about it,
encouraging conversation between
herself and the upper branches

which I can't have, with smokestacks,
ozone on my conscience, complicity
in mass extinctions.

Can I save the woods where birds live,
Grampy? —me and Milo and Penny?
I don't know, Emma. Try it.

Goodness Knows…

…that those helmeted nuisances
at roadside construction sites
who signal two lanes of traffic,
Stop or Slow, are somebodies too.

…that the little girl will spill
her chocolate milk. She does not
mean to: such tiny eager hands…

…that the boggy area near
the tracks, where old tires go
to die, will sound much like Eden,
once April peepers chime.

…that the cat will shed, the dog
make doggy odors—while we,
higher species, also have much
to be loved in spite of.

…that after we beg somebody
not to leave, and they do, there will
come another chance to be happy,

though everyone ends up a sunset
or sunrise short in the accounting.

Learning Late

Why, love is easy, you discover
after a lifetime blocking that route
with boulders and trunks of trees:
simply remove debris you put there
yourself, and the road is level,
straight to the homestead.

Bless us, it is better to learn
just before the sun sets what day it is,
than not at all. Impious old
Uncle Charles took Jesus as Savior
mere minutes before he died.
Pastor was very happy.

Knowledge of what a sparrow means
by singing earns you no interest,
so acquire it only when you're ready.
Something the young don't realize:
late learnings lack years to congeal
into dogma, the way arteries harden.

Mistakes make good students—
and that school is always in session.
It isn't necessary that you graduate:
even your teachers are still learning.

Some say the greatest lessons come
after Pastor throws dirt on the coffin.
Shut your eyes, keep the mind open.

Go Out and Play

To the diffident little boy who is my soul:
birches hold out their arms to you,
black flies can hardly wait—it's all good—
go. Put on your shoes. Go out.

Wear a T-shirt that tells who you are.
You like girls, but don't choose to be a man
in a pickup truck with gunrack. It's okay,
there is room for you, go out and play.

Stroke that Retriever who knocked
you flat last time, out of doggy enthusiasm
and general joie de vivre. He is still
learning how to be tolerable. Help him.

Go out there. The horizon wants you
in the middle. A White-Throated Sparrow
will share its loneliness with a boy
who understands what it is singing about.

Play, where tall pines amble downhill
to the river they love to watch move along.
Join them in looking both directions:
many a lesson there if you're open to them.

Taste the sky, then come and tell me
what flavor blue is. I've eaten too much
earth and stone in my day. Overdid it.
I've long waited to hear how the sky tastes.

*So to you, Friend, I confide my secret.
That's the world, and we all live there.*
      —William Stafford

Telling Time

Wild blueberries on the Turtleback ledges
have ripened green to blue. It's called July.

Fireflies blink the brevity of life
all night. The summer constellations arrive
punctually, like well-run trains.

Milkweed draws Monarchs, first meal
for their caterpillars. Timing isn't everything;
it's the only thing.

New Hampshire was far from Connecticut
before highways, the lake a mirage

at imagination's limit. In the back seat
of the Plymouth: When will we get there?
Little boy, little existentialist.

Aunt Eloise gave up her driver's license.
Don ill with cancer finally stopped eating.

Time seemed an open secret they both knew.

Patience

I nearly stepped on you, crossing the little plot
in the woods, fenced with stone, your name
etched in stone above two dates; your sleep
since 1846 a testimony to your name.

Why did parents do that (fashionable once,
I know): give infants names that straitjacketed
young lives? Stomp your foot, and Mother
shakes a finger at you: "Patience!"

Endless waiting for your birthday, for spring,
for O-Be-Joyful to grow up from playmate
to helpmate (he died too soon), yourself
to become a woman, Jesus to come again.

Not your turn at hopscotch. Do not let
your tummy rumble, until Papa gets to his
Amen at last and slices the turkey. Watch
for the snow-storm of apple-blossoms.

Pastor told you children about heaven:
golden streets, wings for the well-behaved.
I did the arithmetic: you died at twelve.
Couldn't wait, could you, Patience?

Good Listener

Wind catches branches in the Ossipees:
I have mistaken their chafing
for a small child lost in the hardwood.

I used to hear voices in the static
between radio stations. No one special—
just souls trying to talk to someone.

They came in like a woman on the phone,
a man after cigars from the tobacconist.
Where they were, static was the medium.

Now, when a voice starts from branches
scraped together by a breeze, I pause.
It could be my voice up there one day.

I heed brooks in spring runoff,
just in case. It's what the Original People
did, if ancestors spoke from the water.

No need to answer. In creaking branches,
rushing brooks, the rumor passes
spirit to spirit—"A live one is listening."

"But Some Doubted"

Perched on a branch was one owl
the mouse never saw coming which is why
tiny tracks on snow end just here

The owl was culpable of nothing except
acting owlish yet we with our own
footprints to leave still glanced upward

aware that pestilence stalked in darkness
while bullets flew by daylight
We scanned treetops and watched our step

In Sunday School it was taught how angels
had been given charge of us under
whose wings we would always find refuge

Our sweet lady teacher was so convincing
we ran home joyous to tell Mom
about it then saw something in her face

Binocular Vision

Once however rarely in the expansiveness
of vision allowed us for taking in panoramas
of fall color proudly as if it were banners

once in a golden season focus must narrow
to the particular the easily overlooked
Today in fact the tiniest of sparrows sat

uncharacteristically still beside a nearby
house foundation and from my window I saw
every now and then it would flutter a bit

but go nowhere suggesting a broken wing
possibly a window collision which happens in
the hapless lives of birds and if so past helping

While we know God's eye is on the sparrow
there's no recourse to miracles so God and I
just kept an eye on one life so small so small

When to Head for the Hills

You know it's time to take a walk
when friends looking at your eyes
see two iPad screens.

Or people who have heard
the White-Throated Sparrow sing
smile sympathetically at you.

When there is thunder
in the hills, that could be the call.

With moose getting scarce,
various wildflowers endangered,
you'd better get up there.

It is time, when you feel a yen
to turn off GPS and bushwhack.

When you long to inhale a pine
forest that doesn't spray
from a can in the bathroom.

When you lack a good place
to shed your old snakeskin.

When you can't see
your belt for your belly.

Winter Solstice
in defense of darkness

The shortest day sinks into melancholy.
We fault the darkness, impatient for June
and its generosity of sunlight.

Now really. The solstice prolongs rest
for horses in splintered stable stalls,
for nursing home residents who wrestle
with complexities of a medicated day,
for children teased at recess.

There is leeway for dreaming
of trivial events in nondescript locales
which achieve fruition in fullness
of time—like a seed that, some spring,
will offer nests its towering sanctuary.

Time to reclaim from forgetfulness
what was lost during brief childhoods,
long marriages, chronic illnesses.

In the year's extended night, a trinity
of travelers from east of everyplace
have latitude to run their star to earth.

When Snow Falls from Trees in Sunlight

For a long moment, immune to gravity,
a white curtain hangs in the lower air.

There are vapors, curtains, in high places
usually closed against us. We encroach
at risk, given that we are transient,

and that hills alter those who climb them.
Such is the caution. Some turn around,
retreat to places where trees don't grow;

others part the veil and haven't been
seen since—though if you dare the ways
they went, you might have an apparition
of bodiless faces, hear fading voices.

When snow falls from trees in sunlight
before us, this warning phenomenon
will be reported at dinner: "We heeded
the portent, and went no farther."

Hibernation

Is there a better way to winter out
than that of our mammalian kin

They let the white sleep tuck them secure
in dens or crevasses their heartbeats slow

We know how black bear sows wake briefly
to find they've given birth then return
to ursine dreams while their hairless cubs
grunt snuggle and nurse in the year's darkness

Outside a new nature awaits birth and
the bears' emergence like those departed souls
who always trusted their graves
would crack open at the Great Springtime
vernal restoration easily doubted

when caught in the dark of winter solstice
less day than night our cemetery
unplowed for visitation but our widows
with memories watchful and waiting
outside the gates in their long heavy coats

Heart Defect

I was en route down the Cutoff
as a stocky young man hiked up, he heading
for the volcanic rockpile, I for home.

We talked briefly about other igneous ranges,
abandoned mines and mills,
the unoriginality of multiple Sugar Loafs.

I remarked you could drop New Hampshire
into say Texas and never find it, yet
there remains a lifetime of things to see here.

Resuming his climb, he said: "As long as we
can keep those _____ people out."

His back to me, I missed what kind of people
were apt for exclusion—in fact
didn't care to know. I could be one of them,

just don't look the part. I reflect often upon
that stocky young man, building
his walls, guarding rocks and abandonments

for stocky young men like himself.
I think a hateful heart must be defective.

Specimen Owl

Docent shows him to children
under the summer-vacation sun.
A cord attaches to one talon.

Injured past chance of survival
in the wild, his life now tweaks
school-age attention deficit.

A chipmunk runs under a bush.
No need to strain at the cord:
meals provided free of charge.

His head turns widely; she says
a horned owl's eyes don't move
like ours. No sidelong glances.

To meet his unblinking gaze
is hard for me, representative
of an entire suspect species:

little lower than angels to
our own eyes, but spoilage
of habitat on our record.

These children now scatter
in their transient innocence,
to view, before closing time,

a listless coyote, indifferent
bear, neurotic mountain lion,
one-eyed interned deer.

Ignored by a Chickadee

Among snubs collected in a life
of putting myself out there, this

is minor: a black-capped extravert
pecks diligently at the leaf mold
within a pace of my hiker's boots,
ignoring me and my propensities.

Weighed against fall's fat-storage,
I am of course nothing—plus
in a crisis there are always wings.

This discipline of standing still
long enough gives other dwellers
in the arboreal city time to forget
I'm here: in nature the motionless

is invisible. Chipmunks overrun
your boots. A fox comes sniffing
right up to your trouser leg. It is
a benefaction, but hunters use it.

One step betrays me. Chickadee
flutters up to safety when I move
along, lest I be missed at home.

Abandoned Nests

Gazing up into branches fully green
I will sometimes see one blot
of nest forsaken now like a cellar hole
sunk in underbrush the nestlings

fledged or eaten parents flown or fallen
nothing new there under the sun
here in New Hampshire where we have
in our woods whole abandoned towns

An old nest may fall from its limb
for a child to pick up and carry home
if her parents will have it or to school
for show-and-tell or an older child

for a science project the wise teacher
showing the class how it was woven
how cowbirds lay their eggs in nests
of other birds for other birds to raise

A light goes on and one little scholar
toward the back waves a hand
She says That's what happened
to me and my sister we're adopted

Teacher clarifies how broken eggshells
under a tree could mean anything

Unwanted Company

When I tromp ostentatiously
with my noise through the woods
chipmunk goes low squirrel goes high
because who invited me

The one dwells amid earth's secrets
and earth's pain its travail as a mother
giving birth how the ground shifts
slightly or largely how water rises
from below or percolates from above
while worms make their slow way
unseeing and unseen

The other such highways as trees
provide and that inborn downside-up
freedom to travel swift miles
horizontal vertical without setting foot
like me on equivocal ground
then when storms come it has a tail
for balance and warmth

I still know all I knew from the start
but those two aren't having it

Overhearing

Of course, the Black-Capped Chickadee
eight feet overhead was not singing to me—
I was only a rootless part of the background,
or a distraction if I moved.

Little to the bird that it was my kind
of music—I too have defended my privacy
with sweetness; put my best tune out
for someone whose name I didn't know yet.

No two refrains alike in the branches,
unless a mockingbird mimics. Each sings
its name. The woods used to be
a teeming oratorio of identities. Nowadays,

I am entering woodlands so still
I assume I am deaf. Could hear angels
in excelsis gloria if there were any,
or a child who thought no one was listening.

The Why of a Pond

Raise earthwork across a brook
flowing down from the higher Ossipees—
soon you'll be catching pond trout.

That's what Gilded Age money
from a brick Boston shoe-factory could do
toward what Eden was lacking.

Emma, six, collects explanations
like intermittent fireflies in a Mason jar.
She considers the Why of the water.

She brings all new information
home. I sit quietly by the parvenu pond,
contrite for my arriviste species,

for a brook impeded decades ago,
for fins kept from swimming upstream
to spawn, for a flooded meadow.

Regrets to East Weare, to Hill,
underwater now; townsfolk bought out
at market rates—and told Why.

Omen in the Woods

My wandering eye in a wandering mind
sighted one early Purple Trillium
beside an Ossipee trail today—the color
of new wine, to this old wineskin.

Why such exhilaration beneath
my usual deadpan? The war did not stop
over three small petals. Neighbors
didn't take down their "F___ Biden" flag.

Blossoms fade fast. Yet even as
a cloud smaller than my hand means rain,
a single flower up in the woods
is an omen, if we count understatement.

I read in it the soft word spoken
when everyone else is shouting, the pup
that looks at you imploringly
out of its cage at the Humane Society,

changing your life. I read the songbirds
that return this time each year
like forgiveness. I read in it the flower
a child puts in the barrel of a gun.

Leaving No Trace

Wet on the trail. My boot-prints
fill in quickly and fade—like memory
of my passing, from the preoccupations
of Red-Eyed Vireo, furtive fox.

Certain walkers of the world's woods
leave things behind they shouldn't.
Others pick up after, making amends—

to the hardwood, to lives hidden in trees
and holes, to the Peaceable Kingdom.

A waddling porcupine doesn't need
to know your brand of takeout coffee.

Neither are nestling and mother bird
obliged to eat seed from human hands
that cage their domesticated kin.

Love that would not interrupt
can longer enjoy the song. It does not
insist on the tune, or whistle any bird
down from its errands involving sky.

Meaning No Harm

A tiny fawn just recently able to stand
wailed in distress at me—never had I heard
such ululation in the hardwood.

And there was the mother doe, farther back
among tree trunks, too alarmed
herself to be forthcoming in motherliness.

Oh, how I had not meant this contretemps
to happen. How I rushed to recede
up the trail into distance and forgetfulness.

I meant no harm, but the next with two feet
might carry a gun. Madonna looks
down adoring upon her hallowed child—

maternal love is his milk and his slumber,
but in their town, outside the door,
Herod would slaughter many to get the One.

Consultation in Season

If I hadn't stood up,
the deer might not have bolted.
Supposing I went out
and sat on the steps, same hour

each day, in time it might venture
closer—cautiously, inquiringly—
to see which kind I was,
and put my stillness to the test.

Unarmed, I would be a curiosity:
"What are you for, if not to kill?
What am I, if not your prey?
What are we doing here anyway?"

"Well, let's just keep meeting
like this, every morning
the Great Spirit gives,
until we have answers."

Crow, Sparrow

A crow fought the wind today
up in the Ossipees where I was walking.
But that wind held him like string

holds a kite. Made a still photo
of a crow out of him, in its willfulness.
I could count feathers overhead.

The crow either found a way
against it, or else made different plans,
involving the opposite direction.

When Marie said she was moving
to Texas, where she has nobody, we
didn't know how to answer—

didn't realize what winds Marie
had battled in New Hampshire. Here
you go where the forecast takes you.

We all signed a card, then Marie
took her cigarettes and unpaid tickets
west, the way the wind blew.

We stay put, not unlike sparrows
in our trees: out-sung by the weather,
holding on too tight to fly.

Leaf-Peepers

Tour busses passing rock our Corolla,
sweet chariot. Peak foliage working south
meets October's pilgrims dieseling north.

If we squint, we begin to see a parable
in those swamp maples circling the wetlands
with heatless fire, each oak a Burning Bush.

"It is as if someone found a treasure hidden
in the hills, covered it back up, then went
and sold everything in order to own the hills."

Long coaches leave afterward with photos
that freeze a frame. We stay to watch
the relinquishment and the sweeping-away.

We see it through to November and beyond,
as we see children grow up and take
our love with them; parent and grandparent

mistake us in the aging of their minds.
Grandpa would be stacking firewood now,
Grandma canning tart tomatoes.

Hanging the Birdhouse

Winter's chickadees—I counted five—
did not disdain the juniper, two months shy
of foliage. Such birds size up

a season quick. If you can tell icicle
from twig, you'd make a worthy chickadee.

Mothers mistrusted we knew enough
to come in from the rain—we were indeed
slow learning to get out of our own way.

Once the juniper fills out with leaves,
black-caps will be ready for what they know
has come. We'd act surprised, as we do
at birthday parties for us that we half-expect.

We will hang the birdhouse upon a branch.
If birds occupy, it'll be too late for Mom
to realize we could accomplish anything.

What Trees See Coming

Trees hold their arms out, for wind to blow
the snow off. It came a long way down the mountains
for this: first apply snow, then brush it away,
like perfectionists impatient with their handwork.

All trees have shown stoic strength against
weather and logging. I may not be in the woods long
enough for them to know me well, but they know
the wind, they know the chainsaw. Well-acquainted.

They do know my people's bones a little: graveyards,
single plots in the forest. Their roots interlace
with those bones, like lovers holding hands; most trees
are fine with that. It helps them hold soil in place,

delays earth thinning out from under them,
till one last blowdown only the tallest see coming.

I With My Loppers

We are cutting back the overgrowth
on both sides of a groomed trail, to reassert
our right of uphill passage in the woods—

aware that bear and deer cross them at angles,
not intent on getting Here to There,
so never lost. On best-blazed and labeled trails
we are forever losing people

overanxious to be home in time for dinner.
We guide most to Bald Knob and down,
yet the Pink Lady-Slipper yearly changes venues.

Even I with my loppers don't quite dare
go wherever the woods take me, mark the place
I end up as my territory; let pickings,
scroungings, and catchings be the table spread

before me in the presence of predators—
till my carcass becomes loam, and my young
do as I, but with no memory of me.

Not Looking for Angels

A pair of herons passed over earlier:
the union two make. You've seen how stilted
they walk, mirroring their reflections

as they stalk shallows for fish—
well, I can report that overhead they appear
as aerodynamic as the Concorde.

I don't look for angels any more.
That's testing. I want to see what's up there
when other heads are bowed.

Perfectly fine people keep vigils
in a way that implies our bluebirds, hawks,
ospreys, aren't celestial enough.

These good folk haven't realized
the psaltery that goes on at cloud level,
or matched feathers to the rainbow.

They expect a Host, and I hope
they get one. Two herons, enough for me:
their flightpath was their praise.

A Stumble Looking Up

By weather's leave today,
I was under a sky whose blue
deepened hour by hour,
as if Gabriel turned the dial—

from robin's-egg light blue
to Chinese saucer glaze.
Every neighboring pond
and lake offered to it.

It became Atlantic Ocean
over me—hawk and raven
were fish for the day,
one plane a sailing-ship.

It turned into the bluest eye,
saw everything, even
the sparrow's fall. I myself
was beneath notice.

When I have questions
I tend to look skyward.
Except on overcast days,
blue is the answer.

And I'm not the only one:
I can give you names
of others out today,
who stumbled looking up.

Belonging to the Sky

Storm clouds slip aside like a shutter
opening to capture by photography
unexpected blue firmament

but our attention is too earthbound
to notice refocus of weather
heavy trail-work in my case or burying
a grandparent in someone else's

We missed the opportunity
to stand straight smiling and make it
a group portrait us and sky

One raven overhead with oblivious
good timing got in the frame
but a raven does belong to the sky
like kid's weightless kites or

connect-the-dots constellations
I may want to belong to the sky myself
someday but for the moment

am all for alcoves of Hobblebush
in the understory and one cellar hole
that has my history and where the vole
goes if it hears boots coming

Turning Back

I didn't quite "make" Chocorua—
got a bit dizzy just below the summit, too much
midair between ground level and me,
at height. I lost trust in my own surefootedness,

so decided to quit. After all, there would be
another chance, better luck with a trail
from the east, and a cold can of Moxie to open
back home in the meantime.

Only a strutting raven, its beak a dirk,
saw me retreat, and what did it have to squawk
about, able to land there off the wind?
Descending, I encouraged later ascendents.

I can glimpse that upthrust cone on the horizon
this very day. The clouds beyond it
model heaven, till a breeze moves them along.
I think of all the places I'm not going.

Not Turning Back

On snowshoes I trekked down
a woody hill I would need to climb back up
to get home—return in my own
Big Bird footprints to expedite ascent.

My downhill tracks were wider-spaced,
of course, and a stretch to match.
(I learned to walk early, but locomotion
to this day poses challenges.)

Outpacing blazes, even the trail
one time, I told myself, Wait: seems to be
a valley down there, not on the map.
No way out perhaps. I might be missed.

An ancient Spirit of the Hills broke in:
"No, come ahead. This is the path
prepared for you before you were born.
Contour lines brought you to it.

"Return is difficult: the footprints
fade behind you. Your children will follow
other trails. All lead to the one
hollow, where I've got a campfire going."

Sky-Writing

That cuneiform script across the blue
this fall morning was geese. Ancient hand:
cursive that puzzled experts, till a kid
came along, and he read it right off to them.

Adults interpret and predict, unless
they can't—then they make complex excuses
about variables, lack of precedent,

ambiguity. These looked up at the sky-writing,
looked down at each other, and shrugged.
One teased a little humor out of the situation:
"Mene, mene, teckel unhorsing?"

And yes, in time a child joined the experts
gazing at the sky—and just like that,
decoded what the geese had said: "Goodbye."

About the Author

Seven-time Pushcart Prize nominee Russell Rowland writes from New Hampshire's Lakes Region, where he has judged high-school Poetry Out Loud competitions. His most recent book, *Wooden Nutmegs* (2020), is also available from Encircle Publications. He is a grandfather and a trail maintainer for the Lakes Region Conservation Trust. In *Magnificat*, his second full-length poetry collection, Rowland "magnifies," in the traditional sense, that spiritual presence embodied by the hills and lake country of New Hampshire. Topography, habitats, and seasons provide abundance, as well as a healing renewal of life.

www.ingramcontent.com/pod-product-compliance
Lightning Source LLC
Chambersburg PA
CBHW060406080526
44583CB00012B/486